目 录

U0107640

新托福写作的 1180 个必备单词

◆ Education

作业 *n.* assignment

选修课 *n.* elective

学分 *n.* credit

教学法 teaching methodology

适应 adapt to sth. / become accustomed to sth.

适应能力 *n.* adaptability

应用 *v.* apply

社会交往的技能 social skills

团队精神 team spirit

独立思考 think independently

辩证思考 think critically

用批判的眼光去看问题的能力 critical thinking a-bilities

在理解的基础上学习 learn things through under-standing

学生的反馈 students' feedback / students' input

（学生）评价老师的教学 evaluate their teachers' performance

评估 *n.* evaluation

通才 *n.* generalist

专才 *n.* specialist

全面发展的 *adj.* well-rounded

领导才能 leadership skills

为社会作贡献 contribute to society

人文科学 *n.* humanities

社会科学 social sciences

理科 *n.* sciences

工科 *n.* engineering

基础科学 basic sciences

应用科学 applied sciences

纪律；管教 *vt.* discipline

自制力 *n.* self-discipline

小（中、大）学教育 primary-level（or secondary-level／tertiary-level）education

职业教育 vocational education（or training）

互动 *vi.* interact

学校给学生的教育 *n.* schooling

家长给小孩的教育 *n.* parenting

学校提供的课程总称 *n.* curriculum

心理的 *adj.* psychological

身体的 *adj.* physical

参与 *n.* participation

干扰（动词 distract）*n.* distraction

记忆 *vt.* memorize

获取 *vt.* acquire

以教师为中心的 *adj.* teacher-centered

以学生为中心的 *adj.* student-centered

熟练掌握…… be proficient in…

榜样 role model

同龄人 *n.* peers

来自于其他同学的压力 peer pressure

（家长等）对孩子或者其他弱者过度保护的 *adj.* overprotective

动力 *n.* motivation

沮丧 *n.* frustration

（某方面的）意识 *n.* awareness（of）

有创造力的 *adj.* creative / original

富于想象力的 *adj.* imaginative

对……非常熟悉的 *adj.* be well-acquainted（with）

表现出色 perform well

为……打好基础 lay a solid foundation for

自尊 *n.* self-esteem

尊严 *n.* dignity

对……非常好的掌握 *n.* mastery

好奇心 *n.* curiosity

精英 *n.* elite

应试教育 test-oriented education

对 …… 上瘾 is / are addicted to …

沉迷于…… indulge in…

发人深思的 *adj.* thought-provoking

无知的 *adj.* ignorant

学龄前儿童或者上学前班的儿童 *n.* preschooler

对读写技能的掌握 *n.* literacy

对基础数学知识的掌握 *n.* numeracy

误入歧途 go astray

给人新鲜感的 *adj.* refreshing

令人振奋的 *adj.* uplifting

给人动力的 *adj.* motivating

很有启发的 *adj.* enlightening

单亲家庭 *n.* single-parent family

未成年人 *n.* minors

溺爱 *vt.* spoil

青少年犯罪 youth crime

欺负 *vt.* & 喜欢欺负人的孩子 *n.* bully

（正式说法）逃学 *n.* truancy

成型的阶段 formative years

植物学 *n.* botany

天文学 *n.* astronomy

培养 *v.* cultivate / foster / nurture

促进学生的身心发展 promote students' physical, mental (or intellectual) and emotional development

给学生动力去…… give students motivation to do sth.

传授知识 impart / inculcate knowledge

灌输高尚的道德观 instill high moral values

给学生以灵感 give the students inspiration

学生对于老师所教知识的掌握 students' grasp / command of what has been taught

就业技能 employable skills

用填鸭式教法教学生 force-feed the students

学生不应该只是被动接受知识的容器。Students should not be treated as passive receptacles of pre-di-gested ideas.

死记硬背 learn things by rote

为了记忆而记忆 memorize for memorization's own sake

责任感 a sense of responsibility

记忆方程式、公式、定理、定律 memorize equations, formulas, theorems and laws

盲从 follow sth. blindly / follow sth. indiscriminately

限制创造力的发展 stifle / constrain creativity

打击学生的积极性 dampen / sap the students' enthusiasm

产生不必要的压力 create undue pressure

塑造某人的性格 mold one's character

逆境 *n.* adversity

鼓励学生用辩证的眼光看问题 encourage the students to think critically

课外活动 extra-curricular activities

学校是社会的缩影。A school is society in miniature.

不遵守纪律 *n.* indiscipline / misbehavior

违反纪律的学生 disruptive students / unruly students

理论知识 theoretical knowledge

双语的 *adj.* bilingual

形容人嘴特碎的 *adj.* nagging

有趣的 *adj.* stimulating

认知的 *adj.* cognitive

监护人 *n.* guardian

指中学毕业当年成绩最优秀的学生 *n.* valedictorian

大学毕业成绩最拔尖 graduate summa cum laude

刚毕业的学生 fresh graduates

（学生）自我管理 *n.* autonomy

启迪 *n.* edification

一门课的全部授课内容 *n.* syllabus

◆ Technology

非常先进的 *adj.* state-of-the-art

尖端的 *adj.* cutting-edge

深刻改变 *vt.* transform

彻底变革 *vt.* revolutionize

自动化的 *adj.* automated

机械化的 *adj.* mechanized

电脑生成的 *adj.* computer-generated

组装线 assembly line

大规模生产 mass-production

省钱的 *adj.* cost-effective / economical

突破 *n.* breakthrough

打破（传统的）界限 break boundaries

无限的可能 endless possibilities

搜索引擎 search engine

信息过剩 information overload

信息爆炸 information explosion

自给自足 *n.* self-sufficiency

虚拟的世界 the virtual world

真实的世界 the real world

（电脑的）摄像头 *n.* webcam

不可想象的 *adj.* inconceivable

远程通讯 *n.* telecommunications

高生产率的 *adj.* productive

可利用的 *adj.* available

新颖的 *adj.* novel

耐用的 *adj.* durable

对用户友好的，方便使用的 *adj.* user-friendly

常规的 *adj.* conventional

增进，提高 *vt.* boost / enhance

加速 speed up / accelerate

生产，制造 *vt.* manufacture

标准化的 *adj.* standardized

印刷机 printing press

电报 *n.* telegraph

外科手术 *n.* surgery

采用 *vt.* adopt

在家远程上班 *n.* telecommuting

网络银行（业务）online banking

交易 *n.* transactions

区块链技术 blockchain technology

提高效率 boost（或者 enhance / augment）efficiency

提高生产效率 boost （或者 enhance ／ augment） productivity

减少人力的机器 labor-saving machinery

取代人力的机器 labor-replacing machinery

自动化 *n.* automation

生物技术 *n.* biotechnology

克隆 *v.* clone

基因构成 genetic makeup ／ DNA programming

创新 *n.* innovations

有独创性的，精巧的 *adj.* ingenious

以惊人的速度 at a staggering rate

超轻的 *adj.* ultra-lightweight

超薄的 *adj.* ultra-thin

便携的 *adj.* portable ／ compact

无人驾驶汽车 driverless cars ／ self-driving cars

器官移植 organ transplant

心脏起搏器 *n.* pacemaker

太空探索 space exploration ／ space probe

载人航天器 manned spacecraft

远程通讯 *n.* telecommunications

通讯卫星 telecommunications satellite

气象卫星 weather satellite ／ meteorological satellite

导航系统 navigation system

全球定位系统 GPS（= the Global Positioning System）

发射台 launch pad

哈勃太空望远镜 the Hubble Space Telescope

防弹背心 bulletproof vest

信息时代 the information age（or era）

互联网的广泛使用 the extensive use of the Internet / the widespread use of the In-ternet

电动汽车 electric cars

清洁能源 clean energy

◆ Media

可靠的 *adj.* reliable / trustworthy

客观的，没有偏见的 *adj.* objective / unbiased

有偏见的 *adj.* biased

有误导性的 *adj.* misleading

报道 *n.* coverage

成为头条新闻，"上头条" make headlines

有新闻价值的 *adj.* newsworthy

信息量大的 *adj.* informative

娱乐性强的 *adj.* entertaining

商业化的 *adj.* commercialized

媒体炒作 media hype

隐私 *n.* privacy

侵犯某人的隐私 invade sb.'s privacy

收视率 *n.* ratings

指某种事物在互联网、媒体或者公众当中快速地
　　传开 go viral

评价过高的 *adj.* overrated

记者 *n.* journalists

新闻界 the press

(美语里一般是指女孩子) 追星族 *n.* groupies

追星族 *n.* teenybopper

文化的象征 *n.* icon

演员在影视作品或者广告中突然成功 make
　　a splash

澄清 *vt.* clarify

审查 *n.* censorship

夸大事实 blow things out of proportion

媒体影响公众的意见 *vt.* sway

电视、收音机或者互联网上的广告 *n.* commercial

海报 *n.* poster

小传单广告 *n.* flyer

大幅广告牌 *n.* billboard

小报儿 *n.* tabloid

有奖竞猜节目 quiz show

真人秀 reality show

情景喜剧 *n.* sitcom

肥皂剧 soap opera

综艺节目 variety show

时事 current affairs

印刷媒体 the print media

电子媒体 the electronic media

报道新闻的机构，新闻社 news agency

充斥着……be awash with / be inundated with / be saturated with sth.

审查 *v.* censor

删除 *v.* delete

暴力或色情的画面 violent or sexual images

被歪曲的 *adj.* misrepresented / distorted

欺诈性的 *adj.* fraudulent

虚假的 *adj.* false / bogus

报道极为详尽的细节 report sth. in graphic detail

夸大事件 exaggerate things / sensation-alize things / blow things out of all proportions

公正客观的 objective and balanced

揭露 *v.* expose / reveal

侵犯隐私 violate (or invade) someone's privacy

毁坏某人的名誉 tarnish (or sully / smear) one's reputation

狗仔队 *n.* paparazzi

名人 a celebrity / celebrities (*pl.*)

丑闻 *n.* scandals

掩盖 *v.* cover up / gloss over / whitewash

不可靠的 *adj.* unreliable

如实的描述 factual accounts

及时的 up-to-date

职业道德准则 code of ethics

监督 *vt.* scrutinize

无处不在的 *adj.* ubiquitous / prevalent

荒唐的，可笑的 *adj.* absurd / ludicrous

高调的/低调的 *adj.* high-profile / low-profile

独家新闻 exclusive news

（明星的）光环 the glitz and glamor

魅力四射的 *adj.* glamorous

处在公众注意力的焦点 in the spotlight / in the limelight

传闻 *n.* gossip

捏造的 *adj.* fabricated

◆ Success

决心 *n.* determination

座右铭 *n.* motto

家喻户晓的名字 a household name

有一定成就的 *adj.* established

辉煌的 *adj.* glorious

绝望 *n. & vi.* despair

逆境 *n.* adversity

不幸 *n.* misfortune

适应能力强的 *adj.* adaptable

名望 *n.* fame

(很高的) 声望 *n.* prestige

名声 *n.* reputation

概率 *n.* probability

残疾的 *adj.* disabled

在某方面获得成功 succeed in sth.

态度 *n.* attitude

毅力 *n.* tenacity / perseverance

一种被证明有效的去做某事的方法 a proven way to do sth.

努力去做的事情 *n.* commitment / undertaking / endeavor

很有本事、极容易成功的那种人 go-getter

很多人都想得到的 highly-sought-after

很渴望得到……have a yearning / longing / craving for sth.

个人通过自身努力获得更高社会地位的可能性 upward mobility

优秀的 *adj.* remarkable → excellent → outstanding →distinguished

意志力 *n.* willpower

挫折 *n.* setback

坚忍不拔的 *adj.* rugged

顽固的 *adj.* stubborn

决定性的，有决断力的 *adj.* decisive

不可逾越的（困难等）*adj.* insurmountable

某方面技能很高 be adept in

不知名的，默默无闻的 *adj.* obscure

身份和地位的象征 status symbol

战略，行动安排 *n.* strategy

坚持 adhere to（principles，rules，a diet…）

竞争对手 *n.* rival

不切实际的幻想 *n.* illusion

不可缺少的，绝对必要的 *adj.* indispensable

深思熟虑的 *adj.* well-thought-out

一无所有到富甲天下 a rags-to-riches story

昙花一现 be a flash in the pan

长处，强项 *n.* strengths

弱点 *n.* weaknesses

重大的过错 *n.* blunder

可以原谅的错误 *n.* peccadillo

有魅力的 *adj.* charismatic

◆ **Work**

明确的目标 clear-cut / specific goals

焦虑 *n.* anxiety

分配 *vt.* assign

冲突 *v.* & *n.* conflict

积极地接受 *v.* embrace

尝试 *n.* & *v.* attempt

竞争激烈的 *adj.* competitive

技能很高的 *adj.* accomplished

在……方面很出众 *vi.* excel in…

蓝领 *n.* blue-collar

白领 *n.* white-collar

谈判 *n.* negotiation

指做某事的方法或者技能 *n.* technique

胜利 *n.* triumph

反馈 *n.* feedback

做某事的途径 *n.* & 靠近 *vt.* approach（to）

工作非常勤奋的 *adj.* industrious

建设性的 *adj.* constructive

压力大的 *adj.* stressful

令人筋疲力尽的 *adj.* exhausting

升级 *vt.* & *n.* upgrade

同事 *n.* colleague

同事 *n.* co-worker

职业发展道路 career path

职业目标 career goal

员工的工作热情 staff morale

团队合作 *n.* teamwork

可行的 *adj.* feasible

非常耗时的 *adj.* time-consuming

妥协 *n.* & *v.* compromise

责任的分配 delegation of responsibilities

工作量 *n.* workload

心理压力 psychological strain

裁员 *n.* layoff / downsizing

尽职尽责的 *adj.* conscientious

招人 *vt.* recruit

激烈的竞争 stiff competition / fierce competition

高水准的 *adj.* high-caliber

重大错误 *n.* blunder

有热情的 *adj.* enthusiastic

讨厌的人或者东西 *n.* nuisance

自我表达 *n.* self-expression

自我印象，对自己的评价 *n.* self-image

自尊 *n.* self-esteem

远程会议 *n.* teleconference / teleconferencing

一种很知足的状态 *n.* contentment

评价，评估 *n.* assessment / evaluation

时间限制，时间上的制约 time constraints

不愿意去做某事 be reluctant to do sth. / be unwilling to do sth.

对工作的正式说法 *n.* profession / occupation

事业 *n.* career

天职 *n.* calling

敬业精神 work ethic

职业水准 *n.* professionalism

很高的专业素养 *n.* expertise

经验丰富的 *adj.* experienced

工作单位 *n.* workplace

企业家 *n.* entrepreneur

事业心强的 *adj.* enterprising

艰巨的 *adj.* daunting / formidable

睡眠严重不足的，严重缺觉的 *adj.* sleep-deprived

（人）闲着的，（物品）闲置的 *adj.* idle

重要性 *adj.* significant→essential→vital

对某种目标的狂热 *n.* zeal

非常投入的 *adj.* devoted / fervent / ardent

高尚的 *adj.* lofty / noble

对工作的满意度 job satisfaction

稳定性 *n.* stability

非常难做的工作 back-breaking work

给人的精神压力很大的 *adj.* nerve-racking

和压力有关的疾病 stress-induced diseases

努力 exert oneself

满足感 *n.* gratification

合作 *vi.* collaborate（with）

工资过高的 *adj.* overpaid

就业技能 employable skills

人际交往能力 interpersonal skills

职业前景 career prospects

职业发展方向 career path

重复性的 *adj.* repetitive

自由职业者 *n.* freelancer

自雇的人们 self-employed people

人员，员工 *n.* personnel

有竞争力的 *adj.* competent

完美的 *adj.* flawless

失眠 *n.* insomnia

加班 work overtime

工作狂 *n.* workaholic

奖励，回报 *n.* reward

激励物，奖励条件 *n.* incentive

以身作则 lead by example

团结 *n.* solidarity

整体性，团结 *n.* unity

苛刻的 *adj.* demanding

薪酬 *n.* compensation

抱怨 *vt.* whine

员工福利 fringe benefits / perks / employee benefits

偏执的 *adj.* compulsive

礼仪 *n.* etiquette

超级忙碌的 *adj.* hectic

◆ Government

实施 *vt.* implement

使……合法化 *vt.* legalize

首要任务 *n.* priority

建立 *vt.* establish

减轻，缓解 *vt.* alleviate = ease = relieve

主管当局 the authorities

禁止 *vt.* forbid / prohibit

政府的税收 tax revenue

民主的 *adj.* democratic

高效率的 *adj.* efficient

优化资源分配 optimize the distribution of res-ources

稳定 *n.* stability

解决 *vt.* combat = tackle = resolve = address = grapple with

严厉的，严格的 *adj.* stringent

短视的 *adj.* short-sighted

支出，花费 *n.* expenditure

社会保障或称"社会保险" social security

老百姓 *n.* citizens

严格地监管 *v.* regulate

规章制度 rules and regulations

严禁 strictly prohibit / ban altogether

严格的法律 stringent laws

强制性的，按法律或者规定必须做的 *adj.* mandatory / compulsory

为……拨款 allocate money to sth.

为 …… 提供资助 give financial support to …

预算 *n.* budget

政府开支 government spending / government expenditure

削减 *v.* curtail

当务之急 *n.* priority

把……当作当务之急 give priority to sth.

责任 *n.* responsibility / obligation

军备竞赛 arms race

紧张与冲突 tensions and conflicts

自卫 *n.* self-defense

国土安全 national security / homeland security

缺乏远见的政策 short-sighted policy

扩张 *n.* expansion / aggression

谋求霸权 seek / pursue hegemony

恶性循环 a vicious circle

地区不稳定因素 destabilising factors

太空竞赛 space race

武器 *n.* arms / weapons

下岗工人 laid-off workers / downsized workers

失业 *n.* unemployment / joblessness

基础设施 *n.* infrastructure

公共交通系统 public transportation（or public transit）system

电网 power grid

石油或天然气管线 *n.* pipelines

给排水系统 water supply and drainage system

民主和开明的政府 a democratic and progressive government

临时的应急措施 a stopgap measure

◆ Friends

兴趣和爱好 interests and hobbies

交换想法 exchange ideas

外貌 *n.* appearance

吸引，吸引力 *n.* attraction

喜欢社交的 *adj.* sociable

社交 *v.* socialize

忠实的 *adj.* loyal

志向 *n.* ambition

陪伴 *n.* company

（人）动手能力强的，（物品）轻便的 *adj.* handy

乐于并善于合作的 *adj.* cooperative

有条理的 *adj.* organized

聪明的 *adj.* intelligent

有天赋的，有才华的 *adj.* gifted / talented

体育好的 *adj.* athletic

无忧无虑的，乐天派的 happy-go-lucky / carefree

相互的 *n.* mutual

有艺术气息的 *adj.* artistic

真诚的 *adj.* sincere

直率的 *adj.* candid / frank

背叛 *vt.* betray

敌意 *n.* animosity / antagonism

靠不住的朋友 fair-weather friend

好感，关爱 *n.* affection

拥抱 *n.* & *vt.* hug

安慰某人 reassure sb.

肤浅的，表面化的 *adj.* superficial / shallow

口才好的 *adj.* eloquent

活泼的，活跃的 *adj.* lively

谦虚的 *adj.* modest

尴尬的 *adj.* awkward

年轻人对自己所处的状态感到紧张或者缺乏自信的状态 *adj.* self-conscious

两难的困境 *n.* dilemma

确定性 *n.* certainty

真实的，真正的 *adj.* genuine

低估 *v.* underestimate

美德 *n.* virtue

永恒的 *adj.* eternal

调解 *v.* reconcile

荒唐可笑的 *adj.* absurd / ridiculous

很烦人的 *adj.* irritating

承受力或者恢复能力很强的 *adj.* resilient

低调的 *adj.* low-profile/low-key

很支持（朋友，亲人，同事等）的 *adj.* supportive

有感染力的 *adj.* contagious

豁达的，愿意接受新事物的 *adj.* open-minded

狭隘的生活态度 a parochial outlook toward life

喜欢独处的 *adj.* solitary

内向的 *adj.* reserved

富有同情心的 *adj.* compassionate

不爱多说话的 *adj.* reticent

让不爱说话的人逐渐"放得开" bring a person out

of his/her shell

自信的 *adj.* assertive / self-assured

容忍的 *adj.* tolerant

机灵的 *adj.* witty

有智慧的 *adj.* wise

体贴人的 *adj.* considerate / thoughtful

善解人意的 *adj.* understanding

某人的本意是好的 *adj.* well-intentioned / well-meaning

口齿清楚的，表达能力强的 *adj.* articulate

很有幽默感 has a good sense of humor

极度搞笑的 *adj.* hilarious

过于自我的 *adj.* egotistical

对于……漠然的 *adj.* indifferent（to）

孤立的 *adj.* isolated

爱慕虚荣的 *adj.* vain

随和的 *adj.* laid-back

非常友善的 *adj.* congenial

优雅的 *adj.* elegant

好朋友 *n.* chum

花束 *n.* bouquet

杰出的 *adj.* prominent

（人）很有修养的，（工具）精密复杂的 *adj.* sophisticated

顽强的 *adj.* tough

琐碎的 *adj.* trivial

◆ Old vs. Young

传统和风俗习惯 traditions and customs

很有活力的 *adj.* energetic ≈ dynamic

有前途的 *adj.* promising

保守的 *adj.* conservative

根深蒂固的 *adj.* entrenched / ingrained

悔恨的 *adj.* rueful

常规，通常的做法 *n.* the norm

做事很主动的 *adj.* proactive

老式的 *adj.* old-fashioned

过时的 *adj.* antiquated / outdated

恶化 *vi.* deteriorate

过时了的，没人用了的 *adj.* obsolete

僵化不变的 *adj.* fossilized

人均预期寿命 life expectancy

史无前例的 *adj.* unprecedented

某事物并不是一成不变的 is / are not carved in stone

不实际的 *adj.* impractical / unrealistic

反思 *n.* reflection

怀旧的 *adj.* nostalgic

空巢综合症 empty-nest syndrome

中年危机 midlife crisis

困惑的 *adj.* confused / bewildered / puzzled

迷失了方向的 *adj.* disoriented

心态 *n.* mindset

成熟的 *n.* maturity

有活力的 *adj.* dynamic

挥之不去 linger in one's mind

退休状态或者退休后的时间 *n.* retirement

退休的老人 *n.* retiree

老年公寓 retirement home

养老保险 retirement plan / pension plan

老年人 *n.* seniors = elderly people

年长的身份 *n.* seniority

尊敬的 *adj.* respectful

明辨是非 distinguish right from wrong

1~2 岁的小朋友 *n.* babies / infants

走路摇摇晃晃的那种孩子 *n.* toddlers

13~19 岁的孩子 *n.* teens / teenagers

未成年人 *n.* kids / children

28

20 / 30 / 40 ……多岁的人们 people in their 20s / 30s / 40s…

中年人 middle-aged people

老年人 retired people / pensioners / seniors / the elderly

祖先 *n.* ancestors

反动派 *n. & adj.* reactionary

老龄化社会 aging society = graying society

松弛的皮肤 sagging skin

历史悠久的（传统或者风俗等）*adj.* time-honored

永恒的 *adj.* timeless

过去的好时光 the good old days

皱纹 *n.* wrinkle

花白的头发 salt-and-pepper hair / pepper-and-salt hair

相互了解 mutual understanding

逝去 *vt.* fade

蹒跚 *vi.* stagger

（已经退伍的）老兵 *n.* veteran

主动努力地去回忆 *vt.* recall

温情回顾 reminisce about…

温情回顾（名词版）the fond memories of…

向……致敬 pay tribute to

贬低 *vt.* denigrate

◆ Transportation

交通堵塞 traffic congestion

危险的路况 treacherous road conditions

公交 public transit

磁悬浮列车 magnetically-levitated trains

轻轨 light rail

有轨电车在 *n.* streetcar / tram / trolley

轮渡 *n.* ferry

路怒 road rage

蛮不讲理的司机 aggressive drivers

不负责任地开车 reckless driving

酒后驾车 drunk driving

肇事者 *n.* offender

通勤者 *n.* commuter

交通量 traffic volume / volume of traffic

交通方式 modes / means of transportation

交通工具 *n.* vehicle

下降 *n.* & *vi.* decline

人口稠密的 *adj.* densely-populated

激增 *vi.* soar / surge

过度拥挤的 *adj.* overcrowded

人口密度 density of population

人口爆炸，人口激增 population explosion / population boom

提高对……的征税 impose higher taxes on

行人 *n.* pedestrian

罚款 *vt. & n.* fine

危险的 *adj.* hazardous

撞车 *n.* collision / car accident

高架桥或者过街天桥 *n.* overpass

地下过街通道 *n.* underpass

温室效应气体的排放 greenhouse gas emissions

汽车尾气 car fumes

汽油驱动的汽车 gasoline cars

电动车 electric cars

◆ Environment

产生垃圾废料和污染 create waste and pollution

污染物 *n.* pollutant

尽可能减少，最小化 *vt.* minimize

倾倒 *vt.* dump

排放 *vt.* discharge

重复使用 *vt.* reuse

循环利用 *vt.* recycle

灌溉 *n.* irrigation

节约（某种资源）*vt.* conserve

保护（某种资源）*v.* preserve

再利用 *v.* reuse / recycle

短缺 *n.* shortage

生态系统 the ecosystem

有益于环保的 *adj.* eco-friendly

环境恶化 environmental degradation / environmental deterioration

当地的居民 local residents

紫外线 ultraviolet rays / UV rays

皮肤癌 skin cancer

防晒霜 *n.* sunscreen

有毒的 *adj.* toxic

无毒的 *adj.* non-toxic

免疫系统 immune system

（人）吸入 *vt.* inhale

负面影响 adverse effects

沙尘暴 *n.* sandstorm

一次性的 *adj.* disposable

生物可降解的 *adj.* biodegradable

协调一致的努力 concerted effort

国际社会 the international community

臭氧层 ozone layer

对……形成压力 put a strain on…

有环保意识的 *adj.* environmentally-conscious

不可逆的 *adj.* irreversible

化学反应 chemical reactions

安静的，宁静的 tranquil and serene

自然资源 natural resources

清洁能源 clean energy

替代性能源 alternative energy

商品包装的总称 *n.* packaging

酸雨 acid rain

冰川 *n.* glacier

融化 *v.* melt

植被 *n.* vegetation

光合作用 *n.* photosynthesis

太阳能 solar energy

风能 wind energy

核能 nuclear energy

水电 *n.* hydropower

雾霾 *n.* smog

有雾霾的 *adj.* smoggy

呼吸系统疾病 respiratory diseases

哮喘病 *n.* asthma

极大的痛苦 *n.* agony

人造的 *adj.* artificial

适当的 *adj.* appropriate

愤慨的 *adj.* indignant

鼓励环保 Go green.

开采自然资源 exploit natural resources

热带雨林 *n.* rainforests

侵蚀 *vt.* erode

连锁反应 chain reaction

蝴蝶效应 butterfly effect

彻底改变我们的生活 reshape our lives

贫瘠的土地 barren land / infertile land

肥沃的土地 fertile land

化肥 chemical fertilizer

杀虫剂 *n.* pesticide

转基因食品 genetically-modified food

增加农产品产量 boost crop yield

构成健康风险 pose health risks

丰富的，充裕的 *adj.* abundant

辐射 *n.* radiation

（多指对环境、建筑等）破坏 wreak havoc on sth.

恶化 *v.* deteriorate / aggravate

生态平衡 ecological balance / ecological equilibrium

可持续发展，不破坏环境的发展 sustainable development

环保主义者 *n.* environmentalists / conservationists

对环境有益的 *adj.* environmentally-friendly

各国必须携手解决环境问题 countries on this planet must join forces

增强环保意识 raise environmental awareness

让资源承受很大压力 put a strain on the resources

破坏自然资源 wreak havoc on natural resources

砍伐森林 *n.* deforestation

可再生资源 renewable resources

不可再生资源 non-renewable resources

化石能源 fossil fuels

消耗（某种资源）*v.* consume / deplete

用尽（某种资源）*v.* use up / exhaust

严厉的措施 stringent measures

某一地区所有生物总称 the wildlife in a region

生物的多样性 *n.* biodiversity

污水 *n.* sewage

气候变化 climate change

温室效应 greenhouse effect

全球变暖 global warming

严重的 *adj.* severe / grave

白色污染产生的垃圾 non-biodegradable garbage

谴责而不是纵容…… condemn rather than condone sth.

◆ **Money**

珍贵的 *adj.* precious / valuable

毫无价值的 *adj.* worthless

不安全感 *n.* insecurity

节俭的 *adj.* thrifty / frugal

（事物）省钱的 *adj.* economical

保持收支平衡 make ends meet

紧张的预算 a tight budget

奢侈的 *adj.* extravagant / lavish / luxurious

时尚的 *adj.* stylish / trendy

身无分文的 *adj.* penniless

昂贵的 *adj.* costly

（商店、餐厅、宾馆）高档的 *adj.* upscale

精致的，精美的 *adj.* exquisite

天价 exorbitant price

高端的 *adj.* top-end / high-end

低端的 *adj.* low-end

好运 *n.* fortune

富有的 *adj.* wealthy / affluent

贫穷的 *adj.* impoverished

富人与穷人 the haves and the have-nots

富人与穷人之间的收入差别 income gap

抵抗 *vt.* resist

诱惑 *n.* temptation

财产 *n.* possessions

崇尚消费的文化 consumer culture

过于物质化的 *adj.* materialistic

地位和身份的象征 status symbol

顾客 *n.* customers

公司的客户 *n.* client

需求 *n.* demand

欲望 *n.* desire

贪婪 *n.* greed

自私而且贪婪的 selfish and greedy

攀比 keep up with the Joneses

妒忌 *n.* jealousy

慷慨的 *adj.* generous

慷慨 *n.* generosity

做志愿者服务，做义工 do volunteer work

慈善组织或者慈善事业 *n.* charity

低收入家庭 low-income families

捐赠 *vt.* donate

看不起 *vt.* despise

贬低 *vt.* denigrate

社会地位比较低的"粗活儿" menial jobs

◆ Leisure

旅行 *n.* excursion

观光 *n.* sightseeing

有导游的旅行 conducted tour / guided tour

跟团游 package tour

自助游 self-conducted tour / self-guided tour

异域风情的 *adj.* exotic

有益于环保的旅游，不破坏生态的旅游 *n.* eco-tourism

背包族 *n.* backpackers

旅游景点 tourist attraction / tourist spot

旅行社 travel agency

纪念品 *n.* souvenir

探索 *vt.* explore

城堡 *n.* castle

手工制品 *n.* handicrafts

古代留下来的东西 *n.* relics

古代留下来的工艺品 *n.* artifacts

珍惜 *vt.* cherish

收藏 *n.* collection

美术馆，画廊 *n.* gallery

开阔某人的眼界 expand one's horizons

抽象画 abstract painting

具象画 representational painting

风景画 landscape painting

静物画 still life painting

人像画 *n.* portrait

雕塑 *n.* sculpture

雕刻 *n.* carving

休闲 *n.* recreation

业余的消遣 *n.* diversion

释放压力 release stress

游乐场 amusement park

主题公园 theme park

从日常琐事当中摆脱出来 get away from the daily grind

放松身心，给身心充电 recharge our batteries

提振某人的精神 lift one's spirits

很值得回忆的 *adj.* memorable

文化遗产 cultural heritage

民间传说 *n.* folktale

少数民族 ethnic minorities

外观，比如建筑的外观，汽车的外观 *n.* exterior

内部，比如建筑的室内，汽车的内部 *n.* interior

化妆品 *n.* cosmetics

业余爱好者，"票友儿" *n.* amateur

虚构情节的书 *n.* fiction

以事实为基础的书 *n.* non-fiction

侦探小说 detective novel

传记 *n.* biography

励志书 motivational books

乐器 musical instrument

音乐剧 *n.* musical

表演 *n.* performance

塑造某人的性格 mold one's personality

捕捉 *vt.* capture

让人放松 calm the nerves and restore the soul

芭蕾舞 *n.* ballet

电影 *n.* flick

演员的表演或者演技 *n.* acting

看了开头就知道结尾的那种俗套剧情 *adj.* predictable storyline / plot

大团圆的结局 a happy ending

动画片 *n.* animation

电影里的特效 special effects

展览 *n.* exhibition

展览或者展品 *n.* exhibit

马戏团 *n.* circus

低强度的锻炼 light exercise

中等强度的锻炼 moderate exercise

高强度锻炼 vigorous exercise / strenuous exercise

越野摩托车运动 dirt biking

适度 *n.* moderation

健身 *n.* workout

有氧运动 aerobic exercises

血液循环 blood circulation

灵活性 *n.* flexibility

耐力 *n.* endurance

协调性 *n.* coordination

马拉松 *n.* marathon

高雅的品位 exquisite tastes

古董 *n.* antique

超级好看的 *adj.* gorgeous

不好看的 *adj.* unsightly

涉及多种感官的 *adj.* multisensory

有吸引力的 *adj.* appealing / attractive

极有吸引力的 *adj.* fascinating / captivating

放纵于…… indulge in...

一个笑话最后的那句最逗的话，笑话里的"包袱" punch line

让人很兴奋的 *adj.* exhilarating

审美的 *adj.* aesthetic

俗气的 *adj.* tacky

乐队 *n.* band

（交响）乐团 *n.* orchestra

交响乐 *n.* symphony

骑马 horseback riding

射箭 *n.* archery

铁人三项 *n.* triathlon

室内自行车运动 *n.* spinning

◆ Family

老年人 elderly people / senior citizens

亲情 family bonds

增进亲情 build family bonds

家庭观念 family values

配偶 *n.* spouse

兄弟姐妹 *n.* siblings

表兄弟/姐妹 *n.* cousin

家务事儿, **housework** household chores

相互的支持与谅解 *n.* give-and-take

家电 household appliances

被……所拖累 be tied down by

代沟 generation gap

导致误解 cause misunderstanding

性格冲突 personality clash

和谐 *n.* harmony

只有父母和孩子一起住的小家庭 nuclear family

一大家子人 extended family

社区 *n.* neighborhood

传家宝 family heirloom

血浓于水 Blood is thicker than water.

社区感 a sense of community

归属感 a sense of belonging

单亲家庭 single-parent households

家庭暴力 domestic violence

毒品上瘾 addiction to drugs

◆ Animals

人类 humans / the human race / humanity / human-kind

(动物园里的动物或实验室里的动物) 被关在笼子里 are kept in cages

给它们造成痛苦和折磨 cause pain and suffering to them

虐待 *n. & vt.* abuse

替代物 *n.* replacements = alternatives

动物 *n.* creatures

伙伴 *n.* companion

驱散我们的寂寞 drive off our loneliness

表现很乖的 *adj.* well-behaved

保护 *vt.* preserve

自然栖息地 natural habitats

残忍的 *adj.* brutal / callous / ruthless

生物多样性 *n.* biodiversity

濒危物种 endangered species

野生生物保护区 wildlife conservation areas

制药公司 pharmaceutical company

生物医学的研究 biomedical research

临床的 *adj.* clinical

实验室 *n.* laboratory

（用实验、仪器等进行的）模拟 *n.* simulation

动物权益保护主义者 animal rights activists

医学研究 medical research

尽可能减少它们的痛苦 minimize their pain

宠物是它们主人的伙伴 pets are their owners' companions

帮助它们的主人减轻压力与孤独 help their owners reduce stress and loneliness

偷猎 *v.* poach

某种事物是没有替代物的 there are no replacements / substitutes / alternatives for sth.

◆ Food

味道好的 *adj.* tasty

风味 *n.* flavor

美味食品 *n.* delicacy

地道的，正宗的 *adj.* authentic

丰富的种类 *n.* variety

有机的 *adj.* organic

摄入量 *n.* intake

……的摄入过多 excessive intake of…

含有过多的糖，脂肪或盐 contain too much sugar, fat or salt

肥胖症 *n.* obesity

心脏病 heart disease

糖尿病 *n.* diabetes

食品卫生 food hygiene

缺少运动的生活方式 a sedentary lifestyle

很不健康的外卖或者速冻食品 TV dinner

心血管疾病 cardiovascular disease

泛指治疗 *n.* treatment

营养成分构成表 nutrition fact

有营养的 *adj.* nutritious

素食主义者 *n.* vegetarian

冷冻食品 frozen food

罐装食品 canned food

防腐剂 *n.* preservative

让人发胖的 *adj.* fattening

控制饮食 watch your diet

对于……上瘾 are addicted to …

从超市或者别的商店里买的食品 *n.* groceries

低热量的 *adj.* low-calorie

低脂肪而且低糖的 low-fat and low-sugar

低胆固醇的 *adj.* low-cholesterol

以不破坏健康的进度去减肥 lose weight at a healthy pace

钙 *n.* calcium

高纤维 high in fiber

发胖 gain weight

超重的 *adj.* overweight

慢性病 chronic diseases

（疾病的）症状 *n.* symptoms

菜系 *n.* cuisine

具体做某个菜的方法 *n.* recipe

饿得不行了的 *adj.* starving

保持体格强健 keep fit

精力充沛的 *adj.* energetic

做菜的原料 *n.* ingredient

饮料的正式说法 *n.* beverage

健康的饮食结构 a healthy diet

均衡的饮食结构 a balanced diet

碳水化合物 *n.* carbohydrate

蛋白质 *n.* protein

维生素 *n.* vitamin

矿物质 *n.* mineral

微量元素 trace elements

对……提供补充 *vt.* supplement

北美写作 172 句型

◆ 前进类 （论证 positive 方面常用）

❶ be supposed to 在写作和口语考试中都可以用来代换 should 的美语极常用表达

❷ hold fast to... 牢牢地把握住……

❸ bear in mind that... 牢记……

❹ There's no better way to... than to... ……是去做某事的最好方式

❺ go a long way 非常有效

❻ It's worthwhile to... 值得做某事

❼ give sb. the credit for... 把……归功于某人，相应的美语里还有 take the credit for...

❽ enable sb. to do sth. 让某人可以去做……

❾ draw on 借鉴（经验等）

❿ boost efficiency / boost productivity 提高效率/提高生产率

⓫ give sb. a competitive edge 给某人竞争优势

⓬ ... is a gateway to... 是实现……的方法（固定短语）

⓭ expand their horizons 开阔某人的眼界（那个 broaden one's horizons 明显已经被北京孩子们使

用过多了）

⑭ is a good vehicle for... 达到……（某种目的）的途径

⑮ generate...（employment）opportunities 创造（就业）机会

⑯ dedicate A to B 把 A（金钱、时间、精力等）用到 B 这个目的上

⑰ shoulder the responsibility for... 承担起……的责任，注意这里的 shoulder 是动词

⑱ pay close attention to 密切关注

⑲ a wealth of... 在地道英文里这个词组并不是指财富，而是指"大量（有益的东西）"，特别是当它跟抽象名词的时候

⑳ ... is a lifelong process 是持续一生的过程

㉑ put... into practice 把……投入实践

㉒ fulfill one's potential 发挥某人的潜力

㉓ from within... 来自内心深处

㉔ remove the barrier for 为（发展、交流等）消除障碍

㉕ be in tune with... 与……一致，与……和谐

㉖ keep pace with... 与……同步发展

㉗ promote the development of... 促进……的发展

㉘ raise people's awareness of ... 提高人们的某

种意识

㉙ ... has found one's niche 找到了属于自己的一片天地

㉚ be the cornerstone of... 是……的基石

㉛ be an essential ingredient of... 是……的必备条件

㉜ sharpen one's intellect 提高某人用知识去分析问题的能力

㉝ achieve and maintain sth. 实现并且保持某种状态

㉞ be a positive alternative to ... 某事物是有益替代方式

㉟ participate in 参与

㊱ afford people the sense of belonging / the sense of fulfillment / the sense of achievement 给人们归属感/成就感，注意在写作里 afford 经常是"提供"的意思

㊲ ... is a main driving force behind... 是……的主要推动力

㊳ reverse the damage to... 挽回对……的破坏

㊴ is a perfect complement to... 是对于……的极好补充（注意：complement 的拼写要和"compliment 夸奖"区分开）

㊵ be in accordance with 与……一致，符合，类似

的表达还有 be in line with 和 be in keeping with

⑪ catch a glimpse of… 很快地了解一下某种事物，像中文的"走马观花"

⑫ integrate / incorporate … into … 将……结合进……

⑬ give priority to sth. 把……放在优先位置

⑭ inject… into… 把……注入，赋予……

⑮ explore every avenue toward… 去探索完成……的各种途径

⑯ awaken the conscience of society 唤起社会的良知或者责任感

⑰ unravel the mystery of… 解释清楚本来很难理解的情况

⑱ Far from being… 完全不是……

⑲ meet the needs of / satisfy the needs of… 满足……的需求

⑳ are obligated to… 有义务去做某事

㉑ make it a point to… 确保去做某事（=make sure / ensure that）

㉒ … is a milestone/milepost in… 在……的过程中是一个标志性（或者更严肃地说"是里程碑似的"）事件

㉓ … is the cradle of… 是……的发源地

㉠ ... take sanctuary in... 在……中找到避风港

㉟ gain / lose momentum 这个 momentum 很像中文里的"势",相应的这三个表达就是:某件事情的势头更强劲或者势头减弱了

㊱ rise to the occasion 这个表达在写作里酷似中文的"迎难而上"

㊲ exude confidence / an air of wealth and power(某人)浑身散发着某种品质

㊳ a labor of love 是指那种发自内心心甘情愿地去做的努力

㊴ get into the swing of things 去努力熟悉、适应身边的事物

◆ 倒退类(作文中论证 negative 方面常用)

❶ be at risk 处在风险中

❷ ... few of us have ever stopped to think about... 很少有人去考虑……

❸ be concerned about... 对……很关注,担忧

❹ have a hard time doing sth. 很难实现或者完成某事

❺ be at odds with sth. 与……不符,与……冲突

⑥ be threatened with... 受到……的威胁

⑦ abide by / comply with 遵守（法律，规定等）

⑧ ... very little, if any, ... 只有很少，如果有的话

⑨ be overly dependent on... 对某事过度依赖的

⑩ be hard-pressed to... = find it difficult to...

⑪ be in short supply 供应短缺

⑫ widen the gap between ... and ... 加大两者之间的差距

⑬ in part because... / partly because... 部分因为……

⑭ frown on... 对……皱眉头，反对

⑮ If..., ... will ensue 如果……，某种结果将跟随而来

⑯ ... hover at high levels ……居高不下

⑰ be inundated with sth. / be saturated with sth. 充斥着……（一般跟负面的东东）

⑱ be subject to... 这里的 subject 是形容词，不是学科，而是"经受、遭受……"

⑲ A can be attributed to B　A 可以归因于 B，偶尔也用于正面含义，但多数时候都用于负面情况

⑳ be susceptible to: 容易受到来自……的负面影响

㉑ distract sb. from... 分散某人的注意力

㉒ at the expense of... 以……为代价

㉓ run contrary to 与……背道而驰

㉔ erode the cultural identity / national pride 侵蚀文化特性 /民族自豪感

㉕ It's wrong to equate... with... 把……等同于……是错误的

㉖ be confronted with sth. 面对挑战，危机，困难等，写作里经常可以用它来代替 face 这个大家最爱用的面对

㉗ copy sth. mechanically 机械地抄袭

㉘ ... is not a panacea for... 某种方案并不是解决某个问题的万能药

㉙ be addicted to sth. / be preoccupied with sth. 对负面事物上瘾，对应的还有 be absorbed in... / be engrossed in... 但这两个后面跟的不一定是坏事物

㉚ drive up the crime rate 导致犯罪率上升

㉛ exert detrimental influence upon / have adverse effect on 对……有负面的影响

㉜ sth. is unwarranted/ unjustifiable 某种做法很不合理

㉝ spin out of control 失去控制

㉞ are not compatible with... / are incompatible with... 与……不一致或不协调

㉟ be likely to fall prey to/ be vulnerable to 容易成为 ……的受害者

㊱ sth. should be condemned rather than condoned 某 事应该被谴责而不是被宽恕

㊲ What's the good of…? 新托福高分范文中时常出 现的反问句：……又有何好处呢?

㊳ live in poverty/ misery/ frustration/ anxiety 生活 在贫穷/困苦/沮丧/焦虑中

㊴ diminish individuals' leisure time 减少人们的休闲 时间

㊵ stifle creativity 扼杀创造力

㊶ be afflicted by 遭受……

㊷ be oblivious to 对……完全无视

㊸ cause grave concerns 引起严重关注

㊹ spell disaster / trouble for… 某事意味着灾难 / 麻烦

㊺ deprive someone of sth. 剥夺某人的（自由、权 利或者某种生活方式）

㊻ take… for granted 想当然

㊼ poorly-informed, uninformed or misinformed about … 媒体类话题常用，（公众）关于某事了解很 少，完全不了解或者错误了解

㊽ A has rendered B+形容词或者名词作宾语补足

语 A 让 B 变成某种状态

㊾ lower one's expectations 降低某人的期望值

㊿ go from bad to worse 越来越糟

(51) There's no guarantee that... 无法保证……

(52) (a certain problem) has reached such proportions that... 问题已经到了……的程度

◆ 中间类(论证不好不坏 / 可好可坏方面时用)

❶ on the basis of... 基于……

❷ are likely to.../ are unlikely to

❸ The+形容词比较级……, the+形容词比较级……越……, 就越……

❹ old and young alike 年长的人和年轻的人都……, 类似的在美语里还经常可以见到 friends and family alike, teachers and students alike 等写法

❺ ... is a fact of life. ……是必须面对的人生(事实)。

❻ hinge on 取决于……

❼ It's little / no wonder that... 毫不奇怪, ……

❽ More than anything, ... 最关键的是, ……

❾ This (trend) is not restricted to... 这个(趋势)不仅仅限于……

⑩ It's rare for sb. / sth. to... 某人（事）很少
会怎样

⑪ It's not uncommon for... to... 双重否定句型，就
等于"通常……"

⑫ ... may not... otherwise. 否则……就不会……

⑬ make a difference 用于褒义比较常见：做贡献

⑭ think in terms of...+名词或者名词短语 以某种方
式思维

⑮ be aimed at sth. 目标是……

⑯ ... lie at the heart of... 处在核心地位

⑰ the proliferation of... 名词短语：（污染，互联网
等）的大量扩散

⑱ in all likelihood 很可能

⑲ ..., by no means, ……绝不是

⑳ are not entirely unfounded 不是完全没有根据

㉑ put sth. in perspective 客观地看待……

㉒ be interrelated and interdependent 相互联系，互
相依赖的

㉓ There's no substitute for... 某事物是无法替代的

㉔ cease to ……动词短语：不再……

㉕ can be traced back to... 可以追溯到……

㉖ It's no exaggeration to say that... 可以毫不夸张地
说……（虽然这里是 say，但这个句型在书面

文章里也经常会见到)

㉗ ... is an exception. 是一个例外

㉘ 怎样说……的重要性也不为过

㉙ a major shift in... 某方面的重要转变

㉚ sth. is consolidating its status as the... 某事物正在不断加固它作为……的地位

㉛ require/necessitate/call for... 需要……（如果主语是人就只能用 need，但如果主语是事情就可以用这三个词表示比较正式的"need"）

㉜ distinguish between A and B 区分 A 和 B

㉝ ... sound as if... 听起来似乎……（其实并不是那么回事儿）

㉞ is an important factor in determining... 是……的决定因素

㉟ Quite the opposite, ... 正好相反，……

㊱ is a hallmark of... 是……的显著特色

㊲ be bent on / be bent upon... 全身心地投入去做某事（可好可坏）

㊳ sth. is inherent in... 某种品质是……固有的

㊴ There's a definite link between A and B 在 A 和 B 之间有密切联系

㊵ sth. is sb.'s stock-in-trade 某事是某人的拿手好戏

④ A create (or bring about/ generate/ breed/ cause / engender/ spawn/ induce) B **A 产生 B**

④ someone would be well-advised to do sth. (= sb. should) 某人应该做某事

⑬ resemble 动词：像……

⑭ ... abound 动词：大量存在

⑮ reflect / represent / mirror / embody 动词：体现，反映

⑯ sth. impels/ prompts sb. to do... 促使某人去……

⑰ an indication of...

⑱ be inseparable from... 与……密不可分

⑲ ... is inextricably intertwined with... 与……密不可分，如果用更地道的中文说法就是 "与……有着千丝万缕的联系"

⑳ eclipse sth. 动词：使……相形见绌

㉑ be mutually helpful / beneficial / exclusive/ dependent 互助的 / 互利的 / 相互排斥的/相互依存的

㉒ is the exact antithesis of... 与……截然相反

㉓ lean on... 本意是靠在某人身上，作文里经常作比喻用法，指依靠某种方式或者手段，有些时候可以代替 depend on / rely on

㉔ beyond our wildest expectations 超出了我们一切的预期

55 take steps / take measures to do sth. 采取措施去做某事

56 convert… into… 把……转变成……

57 be accountable to sb. / be accountable for sth. 对某人某事负责，这个句型的意思很接近于 be responsible to sb. / to responsible for sth.，只是语气更正式一些，而且主语也更多的是 the manager, the president, the administrators, the government, the organization, the hospital 等比较正式的职务或者机构

58 a variety of / a wide range of / a wide array of 各种各样的

59 the whole spectrum of… 其实就是 the whole range of… 的升级版

60 The bottom line is… 根本考虑因素是……

61 Looking back, … / In retrospect, … 回过头来看，……

62 be a watershed 重大转折

新托福作文难题素材库
（66 个高分段落）

◆ 去影院看电影还是在家看

（1）

Few things can be more magical than enjoying a movie in a movie theater. Watching the characters on a giant screen helps us better appreciate the cinematography and makes us feel we're genuinely (≈ truly) part of the story. The booming surround sound* further enhances that effect, not to mention the soundtracks are always pleasantly clearer. Aside from those blessings, we share our viewing experience — the joy, sorrow, frustration, anger, excitement, or thrill and sensation, with a large audience. In that sense, movie theaters are nice gathering places for social events. And although movie theaters actually lure us with a combination of things, most importantly they are indeed places where we can escape from the daily grind of life and get transported into the past, the future or the present in a different setting.

✳ Technology that enriches sound quality with additional speakers, commonly used in movie theaters.

(2)

It's true that today people can see a movie on Blu-ray or HDTV while listening to a home theater system with multiple speakers and munching on homemade popcorn. But movie theaters are evolving, too. In fact, they've never failed to integrate and deliver innovative audio-visual technology. For example, in Disney's *A Christmas Carol*, the IMAX 3-D technology has made it seem as if Jim Carrey would fly right out of the screen, which has definitely made the animation even more entertaining. And comparison between viewing the immersive IMAX 3-D warfare in *Avatar* and watching the conventional 2-D version would reveal how fundamentally technology has revolutionized the cinematic experience. Incidentally, the snacks that concession stands in movie theaters offer are always more than just popcorn.

（3）

I prefer to enjoy flicks in a movie theater, simply
because the psychological and physiological effects it
can have on us remain superior to what we can get
from watching DVDs at home, despite the fact that
there's sometimes sticky chewing gum on the theater
floor. ☺

◆ 大家是否都应该学历史

（1）

History is important as it shapes our nation today. It
is a mirror reflecting us and thus is essential to our
self-identity. After all, the best approach to knowing
and judging ourselves is seeing ourselves in others.
A. E. Stevenson was definitely right in stating, "We
can chart our future wisely and clearly only when we
know the path which has led to the present."

（2）

All students should be required to take history
classes, regardless of their own academic interest.
Like it or not, we're all travelers in time who
constantly draw on our past individual experiences in

judging the present; and if we haven't individually experienced anything similar to the present situation that we're in, we draw on our collective memory-the very thing that we call history. And since we view present occurrences from this time perspective, the past decisions and actions also set precedent for our future options and precautions. Why are we intensely concerned about the mass killings in Rwanda? That's because we know about the atrocities of Hitler and Mussolini. Why are there on-going, concerted efforts to curb the spread of AIDS across the world? That's due to the lessons we have learned about the ravages of the Black Death and TB[*]. And why do we believe lofty statesmen are just human? Partly thanks to our knowledge about Thomas Jefferson's love affair with Sally Hemmings and the impeachment of Bill Clinton. Hence, it seems the American philosopher George Santayana was right in saying, "Those who cannot remember the past are condemned to repeat it."

TB[*]: *Tuberculosis*

(3)

History is appealing. It's the story of a myriad of people, famous and infamous, intelligent and brainless, industrious and negligent. It's the story of what these people contemplated, did or attempted to do but failed. It's the story of what angered, saddened or pleased them. Granted, this story is not always entertaining or uplifting. Some parts of it can be even shady, miserable, heartrending or make us ashamed. But overall, I feel history is fun, not to mention the enlightening quotes and the mini-profiles of semi-obscure people.

(4)

"History will always tell lies", wrote George Bernard Shaw in his play "*The Devil's Disciple*". The so-called "historical facts" are essentially false assumptions people believe to be true; therefore on the whole, history is the subjective interpretation of historical events where bias keeps sneaking in. As a consequence, conflicting versions of the same historical event can often be found. For example, back in the 18th century, colonial conquests were a matter of pride and glory for the colonist countries. Yet if history can be rewritten from the viewpoint of those who were forcibly colonized, it would definitely reveal an entirely different story of invasion and brutality. In 1992, during the 500th celebration of Columbus' discovery of America, in stark contrast to the conventional approach, numerous scholars presented findings about the inhuman atrocities of the colonizers, which appalled many Americans. Such reexamination and reevaluation of history will shed new light on our past and our future.

（5）

History classes are not all they're cracked up to be. In reality, they're largely real academic punishments. Students are force-fed with a bewildering assortment of dates, movements and trends that are barely relatable or relevant to them and taking history exams basically means mere regurgitation of mindless text. The historical figures have had their personality drained away in the textbooks and come across either as being distant and aloof or just as bizarre characters from a costume party. In class, the well-intentioned teacher often has a hard time making history come alive, mainly because it's almost impossible to strike a sensible balance between imparting rigid facts and making history his-story（or hers）that can keep students attentive and motivated.

◆ 学生是否都应该学习基础科学

(1)

Teaching basic science in elementary and secondary schools is essential to fulfilling their purpose of preparing students to be scientifically literate citizens. In the U. S. , it was not until the former Soviet Union launched Sputnik into orbit that educators began to feel that Americans were slipping way behind in basic science education. In a science class, students not only can learn about physical principles, chemical reactions and biological experiments, but can grasp the process of analyzing hypothesis and demonstrating evidence as well, which is crucial to the fostering of a scientific worldview.

(2)

Another rationale for students taking basic science class is although it may sound drab and dreary to some students, science can actually stimulate their imagination because it not only explains and predicts, it can be completely unpredictable and pleasantly surprising sometimes. For example, these days some smart American chemistry teachers even use Harry Potter style magic in their class to show to their students how fascinating the chemical world can be.

(3)

Yet another reason why the basic science class should be taken by all students, regardless of their future career plans, is that it helps young people put science in perspective by making them aware that science cannot provide answers to all questions we humans face. For example, in the U. S. , students in science classes are taught there are generally-accepted moral rules regulating scientific research, including efforts to avoid the adverse effects of scientific inquiries and the ethical treatment of experimental subjects. Therefore, they will understand that even people as powerful as scientists don't have absolute freedom in pursuing their dreams.

◆ 教师是否应该把自己关于政治或社会的观点带入课堂

(1)

I don't see why teachers shouldn't give their own political or social opinions in class as long as they allow opposing voices to be heard. After all, the First Amendment ensures their freedom of speech. And keep in mind that the "Monkey Trial" defendant, John Scopes (*Please refer to the list of examples in Chapter* 6) was never really punished for teaching Darwinism in class. The court ruling against him was overturned afterwards.

(2)

Such subjectivity in teachers' lectures, even when it's flawed, can lend a human touch to their classes and help students better understand that teachers are not really supermen or superwomen, but some people they can relate to, which will surely make them teachers more approachable to students.

(3)

On the other hand, I would say if a teacher uses his/

her class as a platform to promote his/her own political or even religious pursuits, to impose his/her own social belief on the students, or to make the class a process of ideological indoctrination instead of just sharing his/her interesting thoughts about current events with students, then the school administrators and parents should remind him/her immediately that he/she should stick to the curriculum and stop brainwashing the kids.

(4)

We all agree that teachers are just humans. Their own views on politics or social issues may be unconvincing or even biased. But simply because of their special status — the authority figures who give lectures to the kids rather than individuals who are on an equal footing with the kids, their opinions may carry more weight with young and impressionable students than they actually deserve. So I strongly believe teachers should stay out of political discussions in a classroom setting.

◆ 应该先掌握概念还是先掌握事实

（1）

Without the prior learning of concepts, the learning of facts would be reduced to mere rote memorization of rigid sets of data and would serve no useful ends other than honing students' memorization techniques. Concepts, either quantitative or qualitative, are like roadmaps. They provide students with a conceptual framework for them to better comprehend the facts they will deal with. Concepts present logical rules that underlie facts and summarize how facts have been sampled, measured or experimented with. Also, they facilitate students' understanding of facts by familiarizing them with the key terminology and fundamental guiding principles in the related fields.

（2）

The ultimate aim of concepts is to reduce complex realities to simple, easy-to-understand statements that specify relations between variables. Concepts tend to be more systematic than facts and therefore describe things in more organized ways. They are overarching rules guiding or explaining a variety of processes. They are also more reliable sources of knowledge than people's experiences, beliefs or traditions. Some concepts are abstract and provide general information on common subjects while others are highly specific and detailed and can be applied immediately to improve or justify a particular practice.

（3）

Knowledge about concrete facts can really turn theories into things that we can relate to. Without them, abstract concepts would become so drab or even soporific. I still remember how our math teacher taught us about vectors by first showing us a Kleenex box and analyzed its different dimensions. The fact that many things in this world had three dimensions made her subsequent explanations about the vectors so vivid and easy to absorb.

◆ 学生是否应该选择有挑战性的科目

（1）

Learning how to handle academic challenges and difficulties is like lifting weights: The more we do, the stronger and tougher we become. None of us ever wish for difficulties because of the hassle, disappointment and even grief they may bring but sometimes they do come along. Then we can take solace in knowing we have gained enough coping skills before they actually come that will help us overcome them.

(2)

Survey results have consistently shown that students who take advanced algebra, trigonometry or literature courses in high school are more likely to get excellent grades in college. This is because tough terms, complicated ideas or abstract concepts make students more intellectually involved in their studies and effectively motivate them to utilize as many resources as possible to meet these challenges. Also, the more knowledge students have acquired, the more likely they will be able to link the new information to the knowledge they have already accumulated, which will definitely make learning new things easier. Further, the experience of conquering a series of difficulties boosts their self-confidence and enhances their self-esteem. As a result, eventually taking demanding courses will pay off both intellectually and emotionally.

(3)

I admit that giving students high expectations is an important aspect of challenging them to perform to their full potential. Yet this alone may not be sufficient unless teachers can purposefully create and engineer opportunities that can extend students' levels of cognitive and intellectual development. The realities in American public schools simply don't make me think that's achievable. I'm not blaming the teachers, who are generally considerate and hard-working front-line workers. Nevertheless, they're just like pawns in a big chess game: The entire public education system is wrapped up in cult-like enthusiasm for " progressive " child-centered learning. In such a system, teachers, no matter how motivated they are, are programmed to respond passively to requests for information rather than to create needs for information actively. It's almost like a stage where students are the directors, the parents are the producers while teachers are the actors and actresses, the principals and the school board officials being the backstage crew. I would be hard-pressed to imagine that any major challenges can be realistically posed to the students on such a stage. And in many present-day American public schools, the child-centered report cards are just like press release that makes students' academic performance and prospects look much rosier than they really are.

◆ 小组成员是否应该获得相同的成绩

(1)

It's a highly egalitarian approach when all the group members get the same grade for their work. This practice strengthens their sense of "being in the same boat" and thus naturally cultivates trusting relationships. Only through assigning the same grades can teachers guarantee that the difficulties are shared equally among the members and the challenges are met with all students whole-heartedly pooling their intellectual resources. Otherwise, it would almost be inevitable that some group members would hide valuable discoveries as "secret weapons" just to get more favorable scores. Also, a sense of competition and rivalry would linger on if individual members were well aware that they would not be awarded the same scores for their group work, which would definitely cause clashes and hurt feelings.

（2）

Giving each member the same grade is unfair and defeats the purpose of collaboration. It is unlikely for all groups to be composed of students with exactly the same academic abilities or the same levels of engagement. As a consequence, they will surely make unequal contributions to completion of the assigned work. How ridiculous it would be if the slackers end up with the same scores as the truly hard-working members do? Even worse, chances are that those most intelligent and motivated ones will feel highly frustrated as a result of such unjustified egalitarianism and may even become freeloaders themselves in future group work.

◆ 学校教育的必要性

Today, truly well-rounded education holds the key to opportunities and to people's living out their dreams. All school-aged young individuals should set specific goals for their education, such as to excel in their academic studies, to learn about fresh and stimulating thoughts, to appreciate fine arts and performing arts more fully, to get involved in school life like extra-curricular activities, to get prepared for future professional careers or to identify things that they're genuinely passionate about rather than just dabble in a hodge-podge of things.

◆ 学习艺术的好处

(1)

Knowledge about arts and art history can effectively elevate students' cultural awareness, such as their understanding of the historical context of customs and rituals, their appreciation of ethnic handicrafts and their interest in trans-cultural and trans-generational communication. Also, learning about arts can promote personal development. For example, working on a design project in groups may make children more collaborative while reading novels, watching drama and memorizing poetry tend to make them more reflective. And auditioning for a school musical or singing in a school choir may well give young people fresh means of self-expression. In addition, art classes can improve the emotional well-being of students as they offer creative outlets for their energy, stress, tension or even aggressiveness.

(2)

Art classes can bring practical benefits as well, even though they are not directly related to numeracy, scientific know-how or even literacy which many parents believe are essential in preparation for employment. For example, playing musical instruments can train students' eye-hand coordination, which can be really useful for careers as medical professionals, engineers or technicians. Also, pottery or porcelain making can enhance the cooperation between the left brain and the right brain, thereby enabling students to come up with more creative solutions to problems. Moreover, art classes actually open up opportunities for certain internships, jobs or careers, like performing artists, graphic artists, composers and architects.

◆ 竞争的意义

(1)

We are living in an age when the "jungle law" and the "survival of the fittest" rule prevail. Now practically everything must be competed for before we get it. Kids compete for good grades, and then compete for awards and merit-based scholarships. In the workplace, adults compete for jobs, for promotion and for pay raises. In social life, men and women compete for attention, status and even love and romance.

(2)

To compete with others means to try to excel and achieve a sense of superiority. To dominate our rivals or opponents, we exert ourselves and can't afford to settle for mediocrity. The urge to win can compel us to become more original or at least more innovation.

(3)

Individuals, companies and nations all compete with each other. The burning desire for appreciation, recognition, rewards or supremacy may all be the driving forces behind competition. Personally, I believe that as long as the competition is fair and square, it is actually the only effective way to ensure fulfillment of potential and realization of dreams. What we should do is not to blame competition for all the rivalry or confrontation it may involve, but to guarantee that it is played out on a level playing field — i. e. , even though not every player has an equal chance to win, but at least we all abide by the same set of rules.

◆ 科技是否让生活变得更加复杂

(1)

Technology not only makes our options more diversified, but complicates our lives as well. The other day, I saw an electric fireplace in Sears. Just like any regular fireplaces, it would give the users physical warmth during wintertime. But it had so many buttons, dials and meters on it that the contrivance really lacked the psychological warmth sitting around a fireplace with a cozy fire burning could give us. Also, think about the digital books that so many students rely on today. Yes, now we have more alternatives than just going to a bookstore or a library. But that often means we have to sacrifice the simple leisure of curling up with a good book. Instead, to stare at the computer screen and scroll the sidebar up and down daily, which simply hurts our eyes and makes our neck stiffen. Likewise, inventions like the electronic keyboard, PSP and Blackberry really make our lives unnecessarily complex and drag us away from the simple enjoyment of playing the piano, building sandcastles or writing letters to our loved ones.

(2)

On a more spiritual level, with the boom of technological innovations, the computer-enhanced productivity, the computer-boosted mechanical precision and the fascinating computer-generated advertising, people become increasingly preoccupied with material possessions. Technology has, in effect, caused us to be more competitive and more aggressive. Today, insomnia is a chronic condition that plagues millions of people in the world, largely due to the insecurity brought about by the modern complexity that not only means more inventions and more choices, but also means more greed and more jealousy. Technology may bring us comforts, but the breakneck speed of the technology-centered, highly-charged modern life has taken away our peace of mind that has been necessary to enjoy these com-forts.

(3)

Technology is further complicating the challenges confronting humans as new problems have been popping up due to technological advancement and many of them remain unresolved. For example, the waste gas and water discharged by modern factories have been linked to the extinction of many wild species and are threatening the human existence too. Even things as simple and basic as fresh air and clean water are hard to come by these days. Also, the urban expansion facilitated by the advances in construction technology is encroaching on the countryside and the rustic and peaceful lifestyle rural communities represent. It seems true that humans, through modern technology, are getting many complicated new comforts at the expense of the past simple comforts, which may even mean self-destruction in the long run.

(4)

Those who think technology is making our lives more complicated are reactionaries. Yes, technology has brought about dazzling arrays of choices to us. Yet it just serves to simplify things rather than renders our lives inconvenient or confusing. For example, people used to communicate with each other with " snail mail", which means they had to go to the post office, bought a stamp and an envelope, licked the stamp and stuck it onto the envelope before they finally could get their mail into the mail bag. Now telecommunications technology has stream-lined the process to the extent that we're just a-click-of-a-button away from the intended recipients. Also, customized BlackBerry and iPhones enable us to remain on top of what really interest us besides helping us reach out to our loved ones on the go. Inventions like lawn mowers and leaf blowers make our yard maintenance easy and digital cameras have turned the daunting photography classes into enjoyable sessions when we can fulfill our photographic potential without having to struggle with the mechanical details of a camera. Medical innovations like laser surgery is helping doctors immensely simplify operations that once to involve complicated use of scalpels. In short, technology not only brings us more comfort and more leisure time, it makes our lives much simpler than before with enhanced productivity and better reliability.

◆ 科技是否减少学生的创造力

（1）

Three-dimensional computer-generated graphics offer vivid and precise images, which can be really helpful in illustrating abstract physical, chemical and biological concepts to the students. Plus, multi-media devices are mostly interactive, which can stimulate children's visual and spatial imagination more effectively. Also, search engines and Internet-based encyclopedias put more options at children's fingertips, thereby substantially enhancing their ability to come up with innovative approaches to problems-solving processes. Most importantly, modern technology allows school kids to memorize far less, thanks to the ready availability of the information stored in their PC or laptop. Thus, the kids can break away from the restrictions of rote learning and start to think independently.

(2)

The famous Austrian educator Rudolf Steiner once observed, "I've often heard that there must be an education which makes learning a game for children and schools must be all joy. This is the best educational principle to ensure that NOTHING at all can be learned." Today, high-tech devices in classrooms dull the students' minds with graphical teaching where quick answers replace true under- standing. Students are not given time for reflection or critical thinking. And thinking, after all, involves originality and the courage to challenge conventions. In the end, students suffer from intellectual passivity — the lack of desire to explore serious subjects.

◆ 电影应该严肃还是应该搞笑

(1)

Reality is rough. To help us avoid facing reality, comedies sugarcoat the harsh facts for us. By contrast, serious movies tend to show us the reality or the dark side of society and prompt us to reflect on life. Ultimately, reality has a way of catching up with us; therefore, it would be a lot easier to face when we recognize it through serious movies. For example, Clint Eastwood's last movie, the award-winning *Gran Tarino*, realistically depicted the racial conflicts in America. But in essence, it encouraged Americans of different races to grow more open to one another in the new century. Also, some serious movies, such as many historical and autobiographic movies, teach moral lessons in thought-provoking ways. There is no doubt that movies like *A beautiful Mind* definitely showed us fresh ways to understand humanity and ourselves. In a sense, serious films afford us very healthy exercise of the mind and thus constitute a form of entertainment in their own right.

（2）

Comedies normally throw a whole bunch of mismatched things together, thereby producing an outlet for releasing our daily pressure. They are entertaining and offer us good and healthy ways to escape from reality for a couple of hours. Some amusing films teach moral lessons too. For instance, Jim Carrey's *Yes Man* vividly showed us the crucial importance of being true and honest to ourselves in a melodramatic manner. Amusement does not always have to be mindless anyway.

◆ 读写能力在今天是否比过去更加重要

（1）

Individuals today need reading and writing skills to participate in modern society, whether it is to understand a bus schedule or to enjoy a celebrity magazine, to operate a computer or to use a cell phone to text our colleagues, friends and family members. Being able to read and write is fundamental to our lives as students, employees, supervisors or citizens.

(2)

For individuals, zero or poor reading and writing skills may mean low incomes and chronic psychological strain due to the social exclusion that illiteracy can incur. For communities, residents' low reading and writing skills may mean poor school district performance and low property value. For societies and nations, citizens' low literacy skills may mean a serious lack of productive work force.

(3)

The worldwide proliferation of voice telecommunications and digital graphics makes textual communication seem largely irrelevant to many of us. For example, according to a survey conducted by the US Census Bureau in 1960, nearly 77% of American households back then preferred mail over other means of communication. In stark contrast to this allegiance to correspondence, it was reported by NBC in March 2009 that three out of every four Americans today identified cell phones as their primary communication tools.

◆ 年轻人当中流行的网站的利和弊

(1)

Video sharing websites like YouTube are Internet destinations where people can watch and share video clips on almost every topic imaginable, from Cartoons to sporting events, from music performances to horrific car crashes. They create a sense of community — i. e. , they allow us to upload our talents, interests and experiences and share them with other viewers from across the world.

(2)

Social networking websites like Facebook and Twitter actually bring trouble to our lives. For example, our personal information is often misused by companies for commercial purposes and as a matter of fact, these websites themselves are often used for excessive advertising, which makes me feel utterly annoyed. Also, as members of those websites and driven by the desire to become popular, we tend to find ourselves forced to interact with many people we don't really know well and that simply wastes our time and energy. And worse yet, those sites have the potential to turn our friends and partners into nosy parkers and let them get to know things we don't want to disclose to them, let alone the confusion or even animosity that identity theft may cause us.

◆ 参观博物馆的好处

（1）

Today, most museums have a central theme to them. Exploring those theme museums in a foreign country can be really informative and entertaining as well. It helps us grasp the culture of that country, from prehistoric times to the present day, from rites to rituals, from antiques to handicrafts, from food to clothing, from architecture to vehicles, from war to peace-making. By touring foreign museums we can see the origins of things, the historical debris and the facts and factoids about the current society there. They are like encyclopedias about a nation's glories, mysteries and sometimes failures.

（2）

The most essential difference between visiting local museums and reading history books about a foreign country is that museums are not just about the famous and infamous (meaning notorious). Many of them are actually about the obscure, average people-their customs, costumes, artifacts and preferences in everyday life. Besides, today many museums do not just recount things. They are more closely connected with the audience than before. For example, many of them are interactive, through which visitors can feel the local culture even more vividly. Also, many museums offer public presen-tations and lectures on a wide variety of subjects and that makes them great educational tools for parents. Further, the comparisons and contrasts that museum exhibits can present are far more visual and more memorable than the two-dimensional illustrations in any history books or TV shows.

（3）

When I attended the ASU (Arizona State University),

my favorite place on campus was the Art Museum, which was named "the single most impressive venue for contemporary art in Arizona" by Art in America magazine. I still remember all the peace and quiet I enjoyed there, and the exquisite artworks showcased in that museum. And now I still often visit museums when I travel to other countries because they tend to slow me down and calm my racing mind. They enable my imagination to create its own virtual worlds instead of keeping it reliant on TV programs.

◆ 钱应该花在短期享受（比如 vacation）上还是花在可以长久保存的物品（比如 jewelry）上

(1)

I prefer things that last longer because in today's world of breakneck speed, when so many things are technological, disposable or even virtual, more durable things such as silver pendants, gemstones, souvenirs and antiques can slow me down and calm my anxious and wandering mind.

（2）

Initially durable items may cost even more than short-term pleasure such as a vacation. But in the end, they give us greater contentment. They show us that happiness does not have to be fleeting or circumstantial. The contentment they afford can last very long indeed, even a lifetime. Do we really need a gas-guzzler SUV? Do we really need a walk-in closet full of stylish clothes? And do we have to eat out in an upscale restaurant every weekend?

◆ 提高油价是否是解决环境问题的好方法

（1）

Raising the price of fuel will definitely drive up the price of many other things on the market, from vegetables to dairy products, from clothing to electronics, from imported beers to package tours, as their transportation costs will grow up accordingly. This will be a chain reaction that only exacerbates the already high rate of inflation.

（2）

Necessity has always been the mother of inventions. Maybe the demand for cheaper sources of energy will motivate scientists to come up with fresh solutions to the problem, such as the development of more efficient wind turbines or breakthroughs in producing more dependable hydrogen-driven cars.

(3)

Higher prices of fuel make drivers more aware of the environmental costs that driving incurs. There will be less market demand for gas guzzlers like SUVs and pickup trucks. Public transit and the notion of "going green" will be more popular among the middle-class adults and the kids, some of whom will hold the key to the future environmental problems.

◆ 人类今后是否不再需要印刷的书籍

(1)

Computers have much greater storage capacities, which means you'll have far better selections if you choose to read e-books instead of conventional books. And the Internet further expands your pool of information as search engines put tons of data, facts and theories at your fingertips. More importantly, you can download e-books and edit or even copy them very easily.

(2)

Think of all the trees chopped down for the making of paper (Yes. Today, a still very low proportion of books are printed on recycled paper). But the environment should not be something to be subjugated or exploited. Books are by no means eco-friendly when you take into account the colossal amount of paper they consume. Actually, whole areas of tropical rainforests are disappearing because of this each year. And as a matter of fact, information stored in books is not so durable because books can be easily torn, worn out or even burned. I believe books should only be part of our past and present, but surely not the future.

(3)

When you read a book, you never have to worry about the viruses, worms or hackers plaguing millions of computers in the world. And who wants to curl up with a PC screen and read a romantic love story on it? Realistically, no screens today are good enough to avoid glare or eyestrain for the users completely. Even if you can settle for all the insecurity and discomfort reading e-books may bring, it's very likely that you may find the e-books you've downloaded turn out to be incompatible with the software on your laptop. And don't forget that so far, all the devices for reading e-books use power, which means exclusively relying on them is an eco-unfriendly practice.

◆ 可再生能源的优势

(1)

Renewable resources have been the fastest-growing sources of energy in many industrial countries. Their primary advantage is obviously their sustainability. Scientists have been worried that the reserves of petroleum, natural gas and coal on Earth will be exhausted by the end of this century if the world population continues to grow at the current rate. Renewable sources of energy, such as solar energy and hydropower are desirable alternatives to these conventional resources as their supply is abundant and is theoretically inexhaustible.

（2）

Further, these new sources of energy are largely clean, which gives us another compelling reason for phasing out the fossil fuels in the 21st century. For example, wind energy never pollutes the environment as it does not require any fuel like coalburning power plants do. Nor does it produce toxic emissions that cause acid rain, which, consequently, reduces the health costs many societies have to bear as a result of air pollution.

◆ 乘客是否应该为公交付费

（1）

Free public transit will definitely encourage citizens to use it more. As we probably all know, one of the major threats to the environment today is global warming caused by heavy use of motor vehicles in cities. As a matter of fact, the soaring fuel price has been making drivers think twice about their loyalty to their private cars. If all modes of public transportation can be accessed free of charge, more car owners will be won over and go green and more fossil-fueled vehicles will be locked in garages, which will surely ease the flow of traffic as well.

(2)

Fully-subsidized public transit makes sense in that it is service aimed at the majority of the citizens who are taxpayers at the same time. Being available for free to all citizens instead of just to the elderly and the disabled, it will encourage equality in the sharing of municipal resources and promotes easy and laid-back communication between people.

(3)

The buses, subway trains and ferries are very expensive to purchase or to lease. If no users paid for their service, the government would have to rely on tax revenue to pay for it. And with the growth of cities, the transportation network needs to be upgraded and expanded too. Where will this follow-up investment come from? Obviously, all the citizens will have to face increased tax rates if some of us wish to enjoy free public transit. So my view is that only senior citizens and children should be entitled to lower fares, but not completely free either.

◆ 了解时事的重要性（即使它们并不直接影响我们的生活）

(1)

They are always good for a conversation over a cup of coffee. More importantly, discussing or even just chit-chatting about current events with your friends and family members will not only satisfy your curiosity about the world, it will make your mind more analytical and insightful as well. Also, you can better understand the community and city life around you through keeping track of current events happening in the world. After all, they're all stories of people — how people trust, cooperate or compete with, or confront one another. It's no exaggeration to say those who don't know about anything going on in the world may be entirely cut off from society.

(2)

Even seemingly unrelated things are actually interrelated in this age of sweeping globalization. For example, the US-led war on Iraq seemed to have no bearing whatsoever on the lives of the taxi drivers in Madrid. But the following wild fluctuations in the oil price have definitely made them feel the repercussions. And the Swine Flu once confined to Mexico eventually forced so many to be hospitalized or have to wear a mask on a subway train regardless of how stuffy it feels across the world. Being "blissfully ignorant" can be really risky in today's world.

◆ 对动物的研究是否帮助人类更多地了解自身

(1)

Animal research on primates and other mammals has substantially increased humans' understanding of our own behavioral tendencies and the basic principles that underlie our lives, such as the learning process and the sensory processes. For example, recent research of chimpanzees has highlighted the close link between anxiety and physical illnesses. Also, over the past decade, medical research on mice has been critical to pharmaceutical progress in the relief of mental disorders, cancer treatment and the alleviation of alcohol and drug addiction.

(2)

On the other hand, regulations about laboratory animal care should be issued and enforced to ensure the best conditions and the most humane research methods for the lab primates, rodents and birds, especially those regarding the levels of pain and other sufferings inflicted.

◆ 是否有必要经常和家人一起吃饭

(1)

As with many people who have left home, I sorely miss eating meals around a table with my parents and my siblings. Even though Chinese food is widely available in America, I still find myself constantly longing for the food my parents cooked and the experience of having breakfast and dinner with my family. That was when I didn't have to gulp down endless variations of burgers without even chewing them. During the meals, we caught up on the day, shared our joys and frustrations, talked about our achievements at school or at work, or even settled arguments we had before.

(2)

By eating meals together, we learned table manners such as always keeping our elbows off the table and never talking with our mouths full, and also skills like how to set the table with candles. And my parents always managed to surprise us with a variety of colors, forms and textures. We could really taste the flavor of love in the dishes we shared as a family. I feel lucky not having been raised on frozen meals in front of the television although honestly, now I have to wolf down sandwiches while talking on the cell phone over lunch regularly. I firmly believe families that do not eat together tend to fall apart gradually.

◆ 食品生产方式的变化

Now crops can be selected to make sure that they are best suited to certain climatic and soil conditions. Then they can be distributed easily thanks to the advancements in transportation. The refrigeration technology has made possible long-distance shipment of perishable food. Pasteurization helps us keep milk and other diary products fresh for a long time. New meatpacking methods have transformed home-based industries into mass production in factories, which not only exponentially increases the productivity, but makes the processing of meat more hygienic.

自己在家做饭的好处

(1)

Cooking can actually be therapeutic. After a hectic day in the workplace, what a relief it can be to be your own boss and "call the shots" in the kitchen! You can do whatever you want to and don't have to ask for anybody's permission. And you just don't have to be concerned about the food hygiene as many customers do in restaurants because everything is taken care of by yourself.

(2)

Cooking for your loved ones can really strengthen the ties between you and them. People naturally feel delighted and gratified when they have someone they care about cook for them. That's probably how we got the well-known saying, "The best way to a man's heart is through his stomach."

(3)

Cooking can tell a lot about one's personality. For example, those who stick to vegetarian recipes are very likely to be animal-adorers and environmentally-conscious. For real cooking-lovers, we're not just what we eat, we're what we cook as well.

Bonus:

◆ 是否应该养宠物

(1)

Those who detest pet-free lives tend to stress (= emphasize) the emotional needs pets can satisfy. They would argue that we humans are social creatures and naturally crave companionship. Then when human company is impossible, regardless of the causes, pets can drive off our loneliness, make us feel wanted and comfort us at times of sorrow.

(2)

The opponents have some legitimate concerns. There're always stray pets roaming the streets. Take cats for instance, when some irresponsible people find out that these little creatures have such an amazing speed of reproduction and it becomes hard to keep them anymore, the next step may be tossing the kittens onto the street rather than finding adoption for them or sending them to a pet shelter, which not only betrays the affection and companionship that pet raising is all about in the first place, but poses very real health risks to the city residents as well. Even if pets stay with their masters, they misbehave at times, which may disturb neighbors, make a mess of the sidewalks or even cause accidents. In extreme cases, pet attacks can actually kill as deadly germs may be spread from pets to humans who are not necessarily immune to these germs.

(3)

It all comes down to how pet owners understand their

responsibilities. Pets are, by definition, animals that afford humans pleasure but at the same time rely on their masters for food and shelter. So raising a pet is, after all, a luxury. Not just because in most modern cities pet owners have to buy a license for their pets, but because of the love, attention and devotion pet keeping calls for. Keeping pets on a leash when they are outdoors can effectively prevent them from attacking people or wandering off. Also, picking up pets waste dutifully can help clean up the city. And if all pet owners can get their pets the mandatory (= required by the law or the rules) shots (It means vaccines here.) and take them to the vet (= pet doctors) regularly, viruses in pets would be put under control immediately.

◆ 是否应该把动物关在动物园里

(1)

In most cases, it's better for wild animals to live in a natural environment with access to proper food and shelter. For example, living in the wild enables social animals such as lions and dolphins to play appropriate roles within groups, while keeping them in the zoo may eventually cause the disappearance of many traits that are helpful for their survival.

(2)

However, today the natural environment is increasingly threatened by pollution, deforestation and global warming. In fact, most animals live longer in captivity today because normally keepers are available to take care of their health and diet. And if animals are sick, there are veterinarians in zoos to help them, which can substantially extend the lifespan of these animals.

(3)

Establishing and maintaining zoos are a way for us humans to atone for the destruction of the land, the forest, the river and the sea. There have been joint programs among zoos to increase our knowledge about animals that used to live in the wild, such as how to preserve, breed, and care for them. And nowadays, some rare species only exist in zoos, which also makes zoos an essential part of wildlife preservation.

名人名言

◆ Education

"A child miseducated is a child lost. "

— John F. Kennedy

"Don't confuse schooling with education. I didn't go to Harvard but the people who work for me did. "

— Elon Musk

"Education is not the filling of a pail, but the lighting of a fire. "

— W. B. Yeats

"Technology is just a tool. In terms of getting the kids working together and motivating them, the teacher is the most important. "

— Bill Gates

"Educating the mind without educating the heart is no education at all. "

— Aristotle

"The solution to adult problems tomorrow depends in

large measure upon how our children grow up today. "

— Margaret Mead

"Every child is an artist. The problem is how to remain an artist once he grows up. "

— Pablo Picasso

"The important thing is not to stop questioning. Curiosity has its own reason for existing. "

— Albert Einstein

"A child becomes an adult when he realizes that he has a right not only to be right but also to be wrong. "

— Thomas Szasz

◆ Technology

"As we go forward, I hope we're going to continue to use technology to make really big differences in how people live and work. "

— Sergey Brin

"The world has changed far more in the past 100 years than in any other century in history. The reason is not political or economic but technological — technologies that flowed directly from advances in basic science. "

— Stephen Hawking

"The greatest danger in modern technology is not that machines begin to think like people, but that people will begin to think like machines. "

— Albert Einstein

"If a man will begin with certainties, he shall end in doubts, but if he will be content to begin with doubts, he shall end in certainties. "

— Sir Francis Bacon

"Everything is being transformed under the magic influence of science and technology. And every day, if we want to live with open eyes, we have a problem to study, to resolve. "

— Pope Pius VI

"Whenever you take a step forward, you are bound to disturb something. "

— Indira Gandhi

"What is now proved was only was imagined. "

— William Blake

◆ Media

"He who controls the media, controls the mind."

— Rupert Murdock

"When we were building social media products, we forgot the reason we like to communicate with our friends is because it's fun."

— Evan Spiegel

"I do not read advertisements. I would spend all of my time wanting things.

— Franz Kafka

◆ Success

"I hope people remember me as a good and decent man. And if they do, then that's success."

— Tim Cook

"Brilliant thinking is rare, but courage is in even shorter supply than genius."

— Peter Thiel

"Start by doing what's necessary, then what's possible, and suddenly you are doing the impossible."

— St. Francis of Assisi

"You can do anything in this world if you are prepared to take the consequences."

— W. Somerset Maugham

"I have chosen this, that I might illustrate in my death the principles which I advocated through a long life: Equality of Man before his Creator."

— Thaddeus Stevens

"Our life is frittered away by too many things simplify."

— Henry D. Thoreau (the 16th American President)

"Success is the ability to go from one failure to another with no loss of enthusiasm."

— Winston Churchill

"Achievement is the knowledge that you have studied and worked hard and done the best that is in you. Success is being praised by others. That is nice, but not as important or as satisfying."

— Helen Hayes

"Big shots are just little shots who keep shooting."

— Christopher Morley

"No great thing is created suddenly. "

— Epictetus

"The unfortunate thing about this world is that the good habits are much easier to give up than the bad ones. "

— W. Somerset Maugham

"What after all has maintained the human race on this old globe, despite all the calamities of nature and all the tragic failures of mankind, if not the faith in new possibilities and the courage to explore them. "

— Jane Addams

"Nothing can stop the man with the right mental attitude from achieving his goal; nothing on earth can help the man with the wrong mental attitude. "

— Thomas Jefferson

"The problems of the world cannot possibly be solved by skeptics or cynics whose horizons are limited by the obvious realities. We need men who can dream of things that never were. "

— John F. Kennedy

"Faced with crisis, the man of character falls back on himself. He imposes his own stamp of action, takes responsibility for it, makes it his own. "

— Charles De Gaulle

"The way a team plays as a whole determines its success. You may have the greatest bunch of individual stars in the world, but if they don't play together, the club won't be worth a dime. "

— Babe Ruth

"It is our attitude at the beginning of a difficult task which, more than anything else, will affect its successful outcome. "

— William James

"Life is like an onion; you peel it off one layer at a time and sometimes you weep. "

— Carl Sandburg

"I figured that if I said it enough, I would convince the world that I really was the greatest.

— Muhammad Ali

"We must have strong minds, ready to accept facts as they are.

— Harry S. Truman

"A great many people think they are thinking when they are merely rearranging their prejudices.

— Edward R. Murrow

"It is not the strongest of the species that survive, nor the most intelligent, but the one most responsive to change. "

— Charles Darwin

"It doesn't matter how many say it cannot or how many people have tried it before; it's important to realize that whatever you're doing, it's your first attempt at it. "

— Walley Amos

"The ' how ' thinker gets problems solved effectively because he wastes no time with futile ' ifs. ' "

— Norman Vincent Peale

"Has fortune dealt you some bad cards? Then let wisdom make you a good gamester. "

— Francis Quarles

"If I had my life to live again, I'd make the same mistakes, only sooner. "

— Tallulah Bankhead

"One reason why birds and horse are not unhappy is because they are not trying to impress other birds and horses. "

— Dale Carnegie

"Regardless of how you feel inside, always try to look like a winner. Even if you are behind, a sustained look of control and confidence can give you a mental edge that results in victory. "

— Arthur Ashe

"You got to be careful if you don't know where you're going, because you might not get there. "

— Yogi Berra

"A goal without a plan is just a wish. "

— Saint Exupery

"If a man does not know what port he is steering for, no wind is favorable to him. "

— Seneca

"Yesterday is ashes, tomorrow wood. Only today does the fire burn brightly. "

— Eskimo proverb

"It's not whether you get knocked down, it's whether you get back up."

— Anonymous

"We can't get into top-tier or find a high-paid job if we don't try. Those that we think of as being lucky are often simply those who have been willing to take a chance, to put themselves on the line."

— Anonymous

◆ Work

"Productivity depends on many factors, including our workforce's knowledge and skills, and the quantity and quality of the capital, technology, and infrastructure that they have to work with."

— Janet Yellen

"Nothing is particularly hard if you divide it into small jobs."

— Henry Ford

"When I hear somebody sign that life is hard, I am always tempted to ask, Compared to what?"

— Sydney J. Harris

"The best way to have a good idea is to have lots of

ideas. "

— Linus Pauling

"Look at a day when you are supremely satisfied at the end. It's not a day when you lounge around doing nothing; it's when you had everything to do and you've done it. "

— Margaret Thatcher

"Both tears and sweat are salty, but they render a different result. Tears will get you sympathy; sweat will get you change. "

— Jesse Jackson

"Where I was born and where and how I have lived is unimportant. It is what I have done with where I have been that should be of interest. "

— Georgia O'Keefe

"In the field of observation, chance favors only the prepared mind. "

— Louis Pasteur

"Work banishes those three great evils: boredom, vice and poverty. "

— Voltaire

"What we obtain too easily, we esteem too lightly."

— Thomas Paine

"If men could regard the events of their own lives with more open minds, they would frequently discover that they did not really desire the things they failed to obtain."

— Andre Maurois

"Change before you have to."

— Jack Welch

"Love and work are the cornerstones of our humanness."

— Sigmund Freud

"When you're following your energy and doing what you want all the time, the distinction between work and play dissolves."

— Shakti Gawain

"The really idle man gets nowhere. The perpetually busy man does not get much further."

— Sir Heneage Ogilivie

"Never fail to know that if you are doing all the

talking, you are boring somebody. "

— Helen Gurley Brown

"I can think about money as something that helps me do good things for myself and others, not as a goal in itself. "

— Anonymous

◆ Government

"Millions of individuals making their own decisions in the marketplace will always allocate resources better than any centralized government. "

— Ronald Reagan

"The problem is not that people are taxed too little, but that the government spends too much. "

— Ronald Reagan

"The will of the people is the only legitimate foundation of any government. "

— Thomas Jefferson

"Globalization is not something we can hold off or turn off. It is the economic equivalent of a force of nature — like wind or water. "

— Bill Clinton

"Arguing against globalization is like arguing against the laws of gravity. "

— Kofi Annan

◆ Friends

"We make friends casually, but once they're part of our lives, we should be careful not to take them for granted. "

— Ralph Waldo Emerson

"Sometimes your joy is the source of your smile, but sometimes your smile can be the source of your joy. "

— Thich Nhat Hanh

"People, even more than things, have to be restored, renewed, revived, reclaimed, and redeemed; never throw out anyone. "

— Audrey Hepburn

"The best way to cheer yourself up is to try to cheer somebody else up. "

— Mark Twain

" Friendship makes prosperity more shining and lessens adversity by dividing and sharing it. "

— Circero

"People offer to share their experiences with us, and this can be helpful. But sometimes other people's experiences can hold us back from trying things that we might otherwise succeed at. "

— Anonymous

"Life is an adventure in forgiveness. "

— Norman Cousins

"Sharing food with another human being is an intimate act that should not be indulged in lightly. "

— M. F. K. Fisher

" We are all something, but none of us are everything. "

— Blaise Pascal

"If a man does not make new acquaintances as he advances through life, he will soon find himself left alone. At the same time, a man should keep his friendships in constant repair. "

— Samuel Johnson

"Every man takes the limits of his own field of vision for the limits of the world."

— Arthur Schopenhauer

"That is the best — to laugh with someone because you think the same things are funny."

— Gloria Vanderbilt

"When a friends is in trouble, don't annoy him by asking if there is anything you can do. Think up something appropriate and do it."

— E. W. Howe

"Courage is what it takes to stand up and speak; courage is also what it takes to sit down and listen."

— Anonymous

"The more faithfully you listen to the voices within you, the better you will hear what is sounding outside."

— Dag Hammarskjold

"We are all full of weakness and errors; let us mutually pardon each other our follies; it is the first law of nature."

— Voltaire

"I'm treating you as a friend, asking you to share my present minuses in the hope that I can ask you to share my future pluses."

— Katherine Mansfield

"A true friend is the greatest of all blessings, and that which we take the least care to acquire."

— Francois De La Rochefoucauld

"Listening, not imitation, may be the sincerest form of flattery."

— Dr. Joyce Brothers

"The easiest kind of relationship is with ten thousand people, the hardest is with one."

— Joan Baez

"Our friends are both like us and not like us, and it is the ways they are not like us that stimulates and awakens new possibilities in ourselves."

— Anonymous

"Friends of varied backgrounds and experiences make us more aware of how limited our viewpoint is."

— Anonymous

◆ Old vs. Young

"Friends are an aid to the young, to guard them from error; to the elderly, to attend to their wants and to supplement their failing power of action; to those in the prime of life, to assist them to noble deeds."

— Aristotle

"I know elderly people who have so lived in their long lives. Today, they find great pleasure in each and every day."

— Loretta Young

"It is difficult to live in the present, ridiculous to live in the future, and impossible to live in the past. Nothing is as far away as one minute ago."

— Jim Bishop

"The Past: Our cradle, not our prison; there is danger as well as appeal in its glamour. The past is for inspiration, not imitation, for continuation, not repetition."

— Anonymous

◆ Transportation

"We willingly pay 30,000—40,000 fatalities per year for the advantages of individual transportation by automobile."

— John von Neumann

◆ Environment

"We forget that the water cycle and the life cycle are closely linked."

— Jacques Cousteau

"Many anthropogenic activities foul the air, contaminate the water and devastate the forests."

— Newsweek

"Don't blow it — good planets are hard to find."

— Time

"We do not inherit the earth from our ancestors. We borrow it from our children."

— Native American Proverb

"How many times have we walked past a piece of litter on the ground, cursing whoever was so thoughtless as to drop it and wondering when someone would come by to clean it up? It wouldn't be hard for us to bend over and pick up the litter, then drop it in the nearest waste bin, after all. "

— Anonymous

◆ Money

"There was a time when a fool and his money were soon parted, but now it happens to everybody. "

— Adlai E. Stevenson

"Often people attempt to live their lives backwards; they try to have more things, or more money, in order to do more of what they want, so they will be happier. "

— Anonymous

"The real measure of your wealth is how much you'd be worth if you lost all your money. "

— Anonymous

"Money and success don't change people; they merely amplify what is already there. "

— Will Smith

"Only after the last tree has been cut down, only after the last river has been poisoned, only after the last fish has been caught, only then will you find that money cannot be eaten. "

— Anonymous

"When I get a little money I buy books; and if any is left I buy food and clothes. "

— Desiderius Erasmus

"It is more rewarding to watch money change the world than watch it accumulate. "

— Gloria Steinem

"A wise man should have money in his head, but not in his heart. "

— Jonathan Swift

◆ Leisure

"As the traveler who has once been from home is wiser than he who has never left his own doorstep, so a knowledge of one other culture should sharpen our ability to scrutinize more steadily, to appreciate more lovingly, our own. "

— Margaret Mead

"Culture means the widening of the mind and of the spirit. "

— Ruth Benedict

"Arts bring you hope when you feel hopeless, give you comfort when you're anxious and support you when you're defeated. "

— Rodin

"The world is a book, and those who do not travel read only a page. "

— Saint Augustine

"Happiness is a perfume you cannot pour on others without getting a few drops on yourself. "

— Ralph Waldo Emerson

"Early to bed and early to rise, makes a man healthy, wealthy, and wise. "

— Benjamin Franklin

"Nature uses human imagination to lift her work of creation to even higher levels. "

— Luigi Pirandello

◆ Family

"The bond that links your true family is not one of blood, but of respect and joy in each other's life."

— Richard Bach

"To put the world in order, we must first put the nation in order; to put the nation in order, we must put the family in order; to put the family in order, we must cultivate our personal life; and to cultivate our personal life, we must first set our hearts right."

— Confucius

"The soul is healed by being with children."

— Fyodor Dostoyevski

◆ Animals

"The greatness of a nation and its moral progress can be judged by the way its animals are treated."

— Gandhi

"The most important thing is to preserve the world we live in. Unless people understand and learn about our world, habitats, and animals, they won't understand that if we don't protect those habitats, we'll eventually destroy ourselves. "

— Jack Hanna

◆ Food

" Kitchens are hard environments and they form incredibly strong characters. "

— Gordon Ramsay

"What I've enjoyed most is meeting people who have a real interest in food and sharing ideas with them. "

— Jamie Oliver

"His house was perfect, whether you liked food, or sleep, or work, or story-telling, or singing, or just sitting and thinking, best, or a pleasant mixture of them all. "

— J. R. R. Tolkien

"Learning acquired in youth arrests the evil of old age; and if you understand that old age has wisdom for its food, you will so conduct yourself in youth that your old age will not lack for nourishment. "

— Leonardo Da Vinci

"Food is an important part of a balanced diet. "

— Fran Lebowitz

◆ History

"The past is never simply the past. It always has something to say to us; it tells us the paths to take and the paths not to take. "

— Pope Benedict

"History has been written by rulers and soldiers rather than average citizens and it is, for the most part, about follies, crimes and bloodshed. It mainly shows us how self-absorbed humans have been. "

— Thomas Macaulay

"Every history should be written in a wisdom which divined the range of our affinities and looked at facts as symbols. I am ashamed to see what a shallow village tale our so-called history is. "

— Ralph Waldo Emerson

◆ Challenge

"With the challenges we are facing right now, what we need in Washington DC are not political tactics.

We need good ideas instead. "

— Barack Obama

"Failure at some point in your life is inevitable, but giving up is unforgivable. "

— Joe Biden

"Character cannot be developed in ease and quiet. Only through experience of setbacks and suffering can the soul be strengthened, ambition inspired, and success achieved. "

— Helen Keller

"If you would hit the mark, you must aim a little above it. "

— Henry Longfellow

" Don't bother just to be better than your contemporaries or predecessors. Try to be better than yourself. "

— William Faulkner